THE FIRST COLLECTION

A BOOK OF ART

AVERY T. CLEMMONS

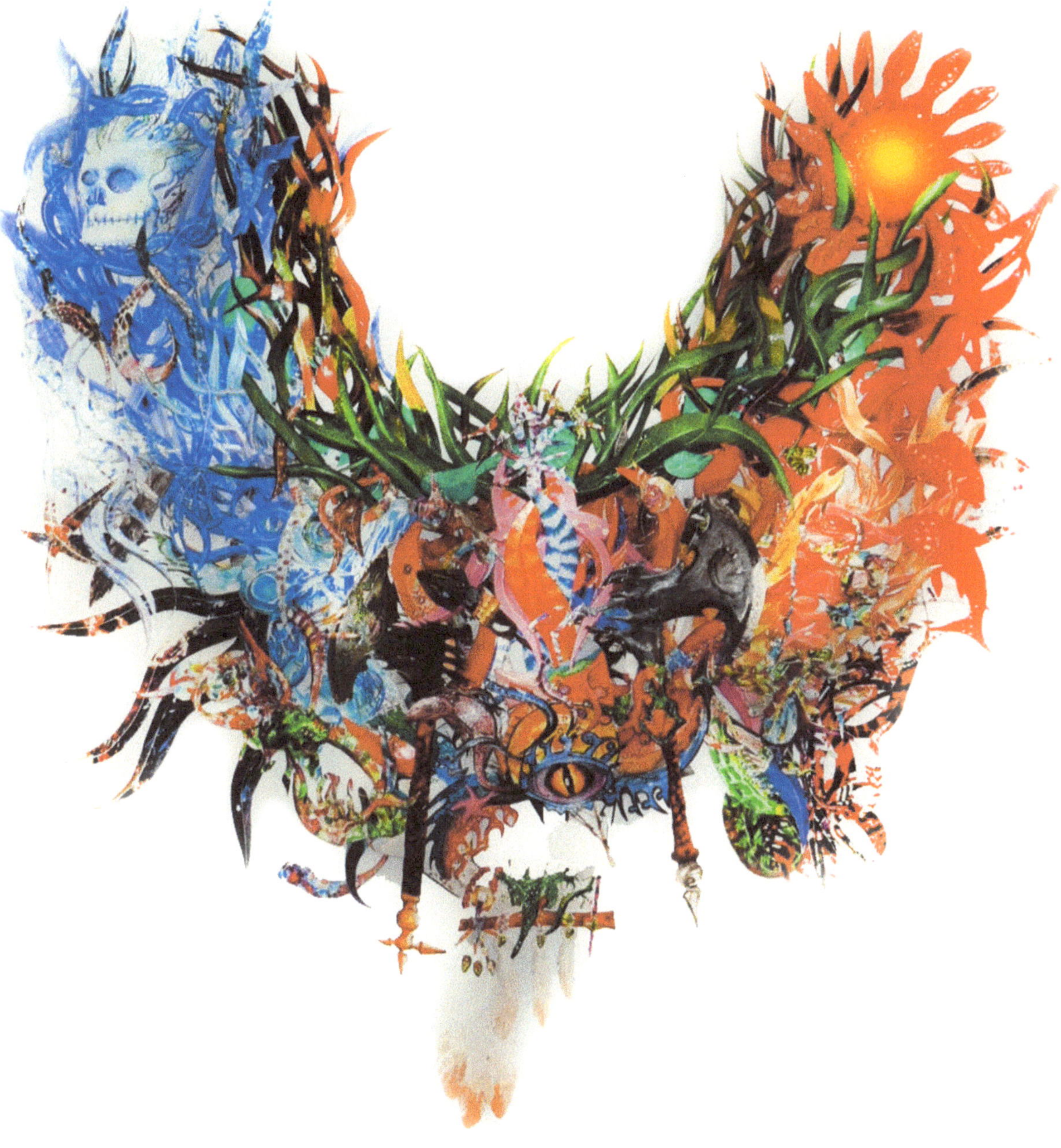

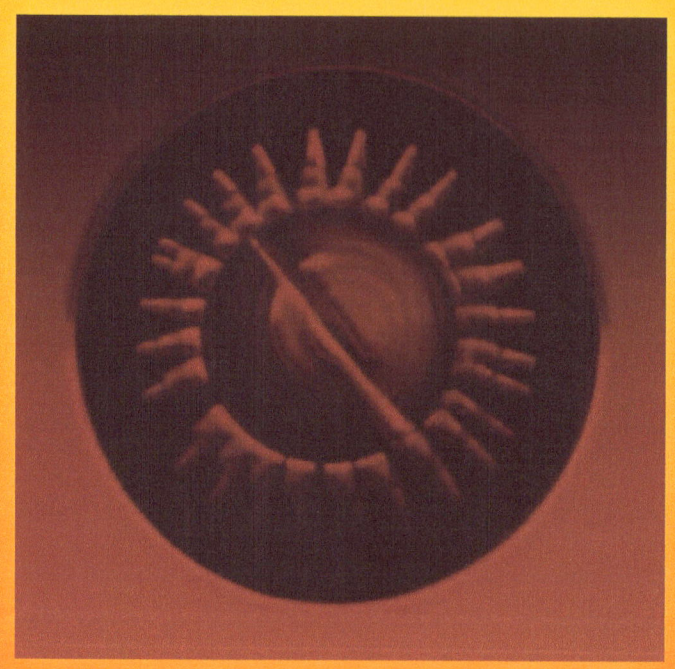

To order additional copies of this book, contact:
Xlibris Corporation
1-888-795-4274
www.Xlibris.com
Orders@Xlibris.com

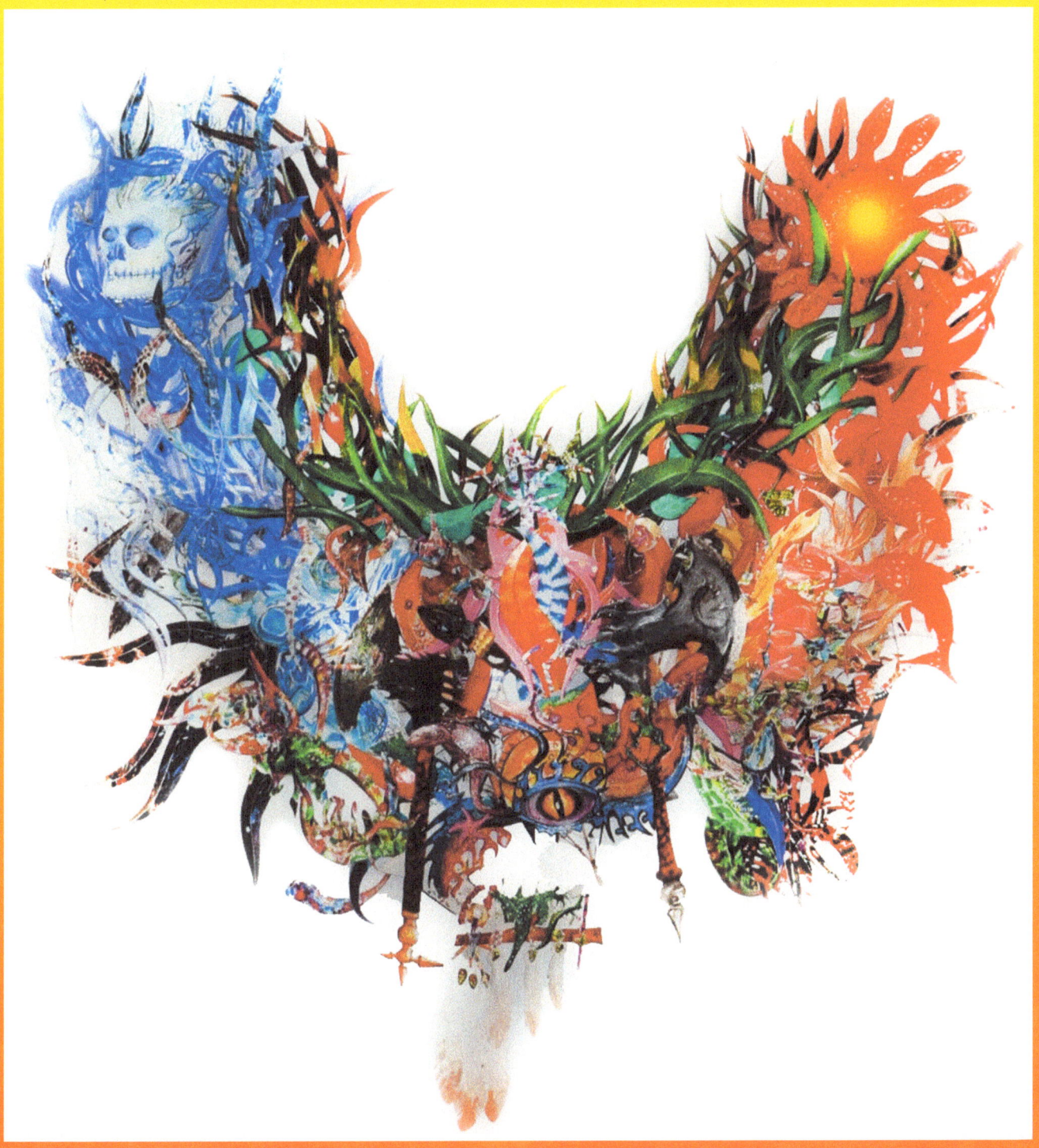

Chartruth

Chartruth is a mixture of native, and yin-yang abstract art. It is carefully sculpted paper, painted with water color and markers, and makes this sculpture extremely detailed. It has a very strong spiritual center full of color and wavy parts. Tomahawks stand on both sides, and beaded feathers hang from a moss covered branch tied to a jawbone. Many of the animals in this sculpture are highly respected and traditional to native cultures. There are fish, frogs, and lots of marine-like animals throughout this large sculpture. As both sides burst upward from the center of the sculpture and change into a water and fire side, it shows balance. The two sides of Chartruth represent life and death, signified with a flower on the fire side, and a skull on the water side. The water bringing forth death, and the fire bringing forth life, is where this piece gets its yin-yang.

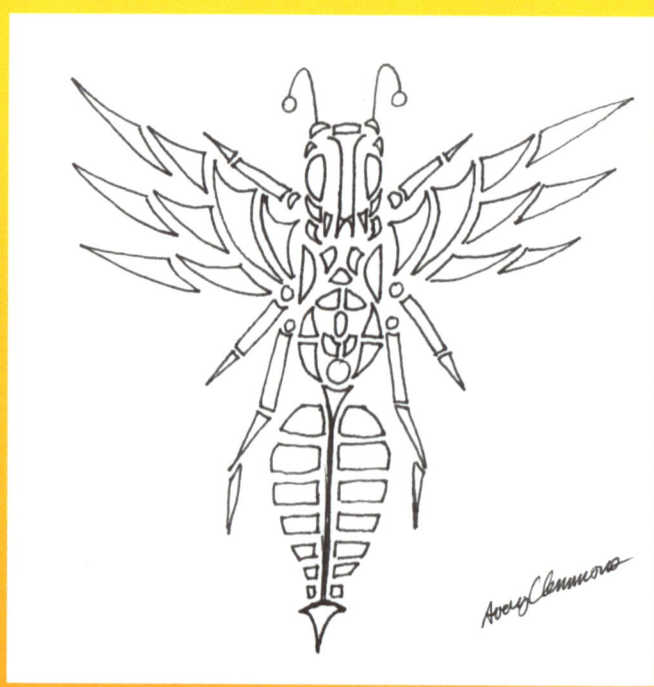

Wasp
The wasp is a favored animal in the insect kingdom, and very common in Alaska. The wasp can sting, build, and likes to eat mosquitoes, and little pieces of salmon.

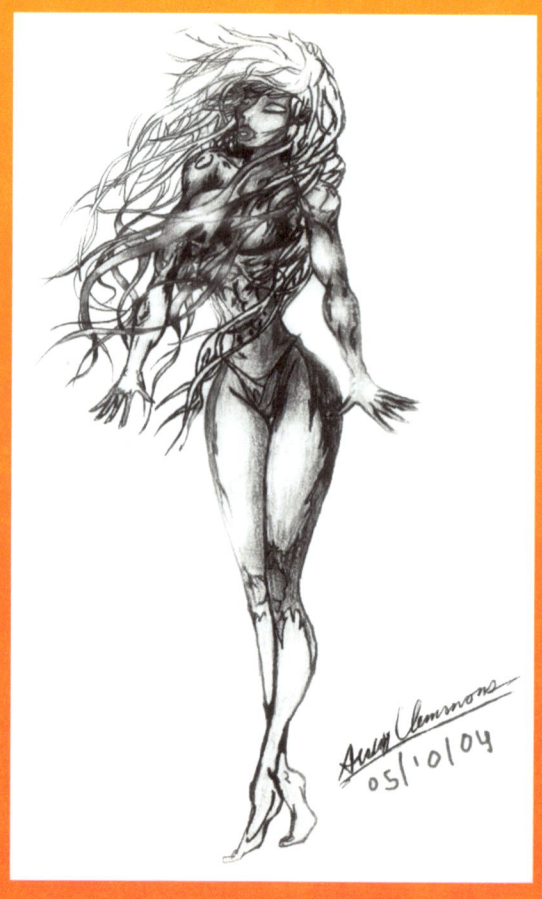

Chills
Chills is a sketch of a woman with a cold bluster of wind coming suddenly from behind.

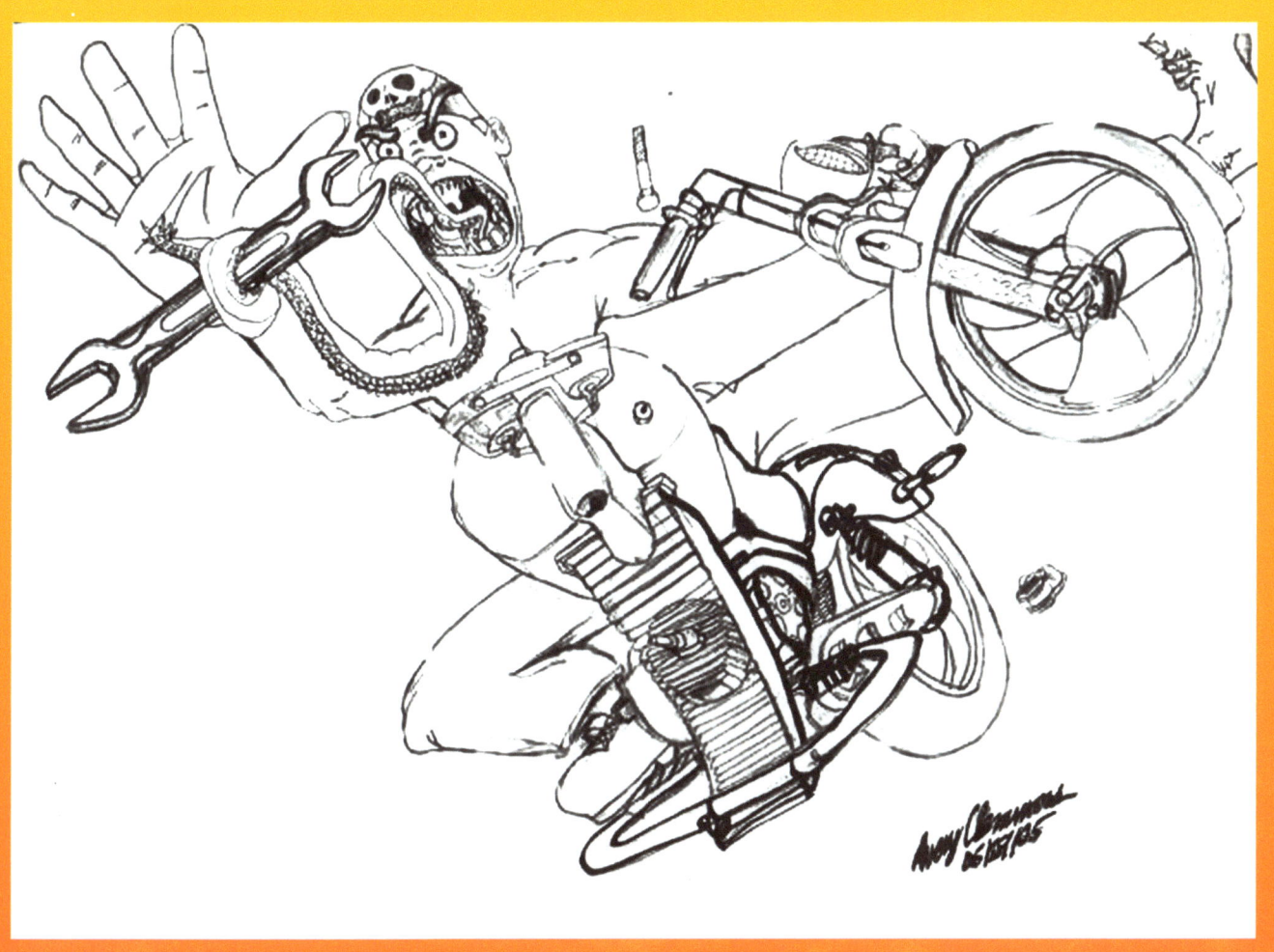

Reach

Sometimes it doesn't matter how hard we try to keep things from happening the inevitable break down will eventually occur. This sketch shows the persevering will of mankind to never give up.

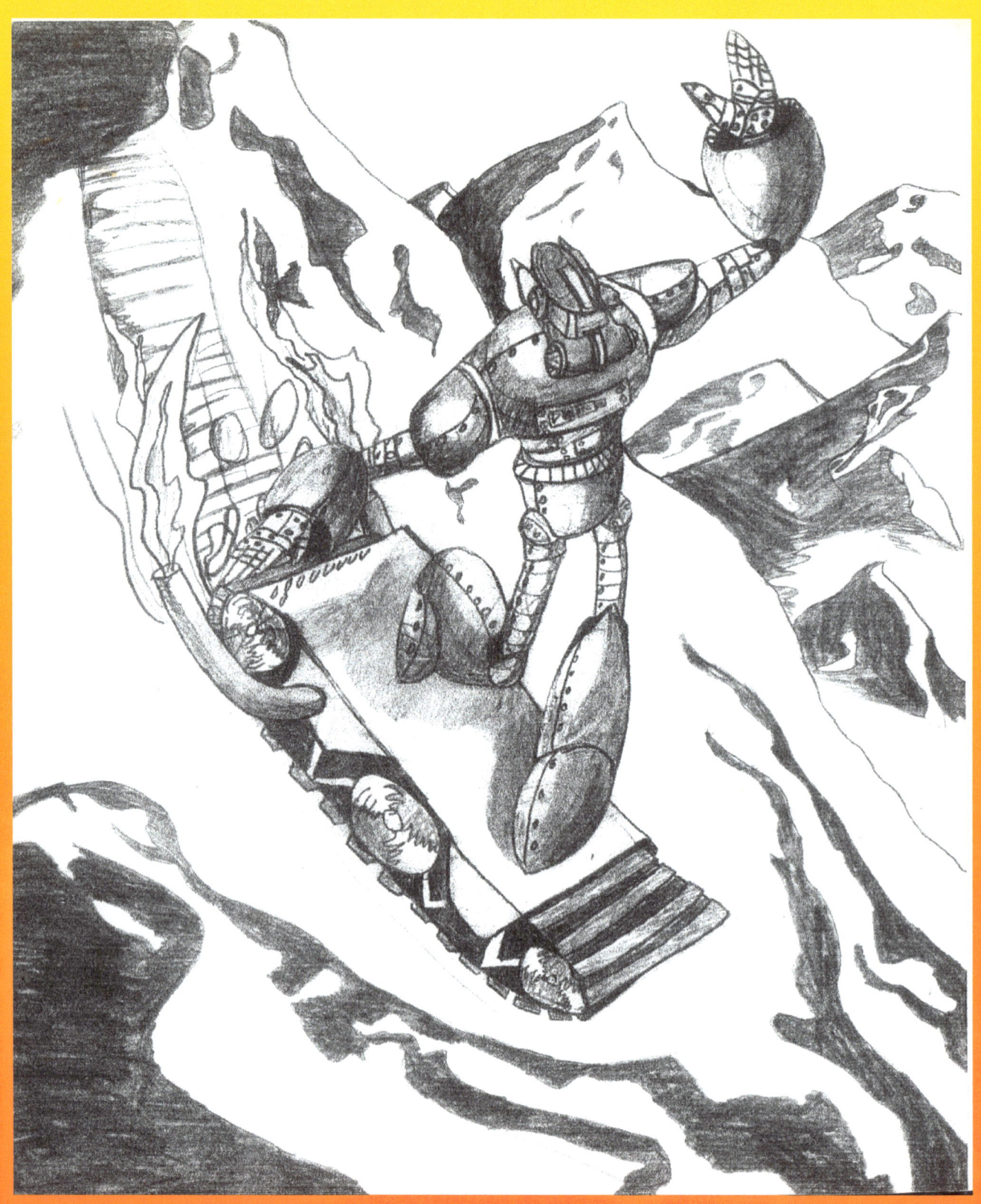

Hot Snow

Hot Snow is a sketch. This robot is having a blast down the mountain on his jet powered tractor board.

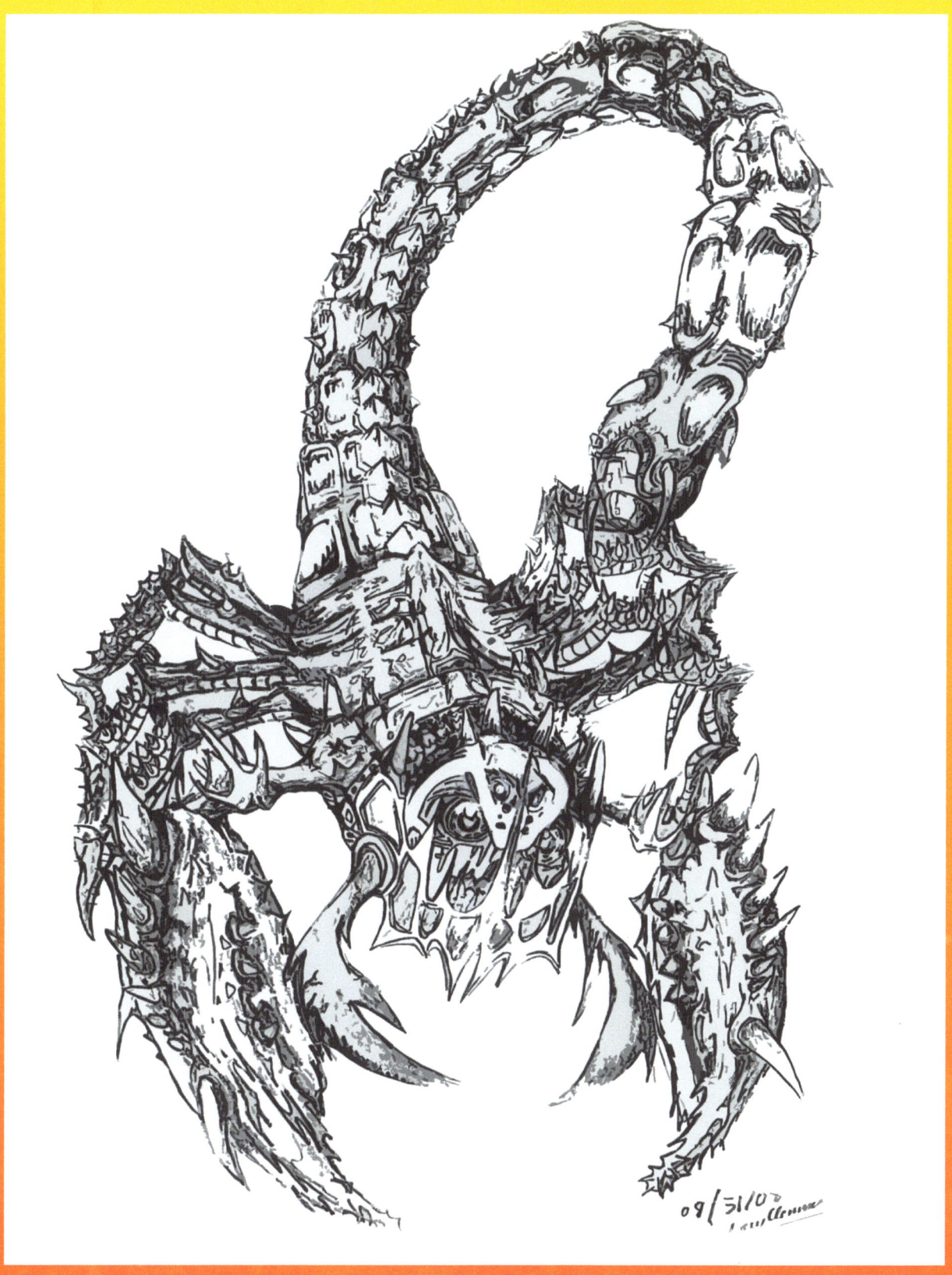

The scorpion

The scorpion is a popular zodiac. The combination of biomechanics, spines, and a laser cannon stinger give this picture a real warrior style.

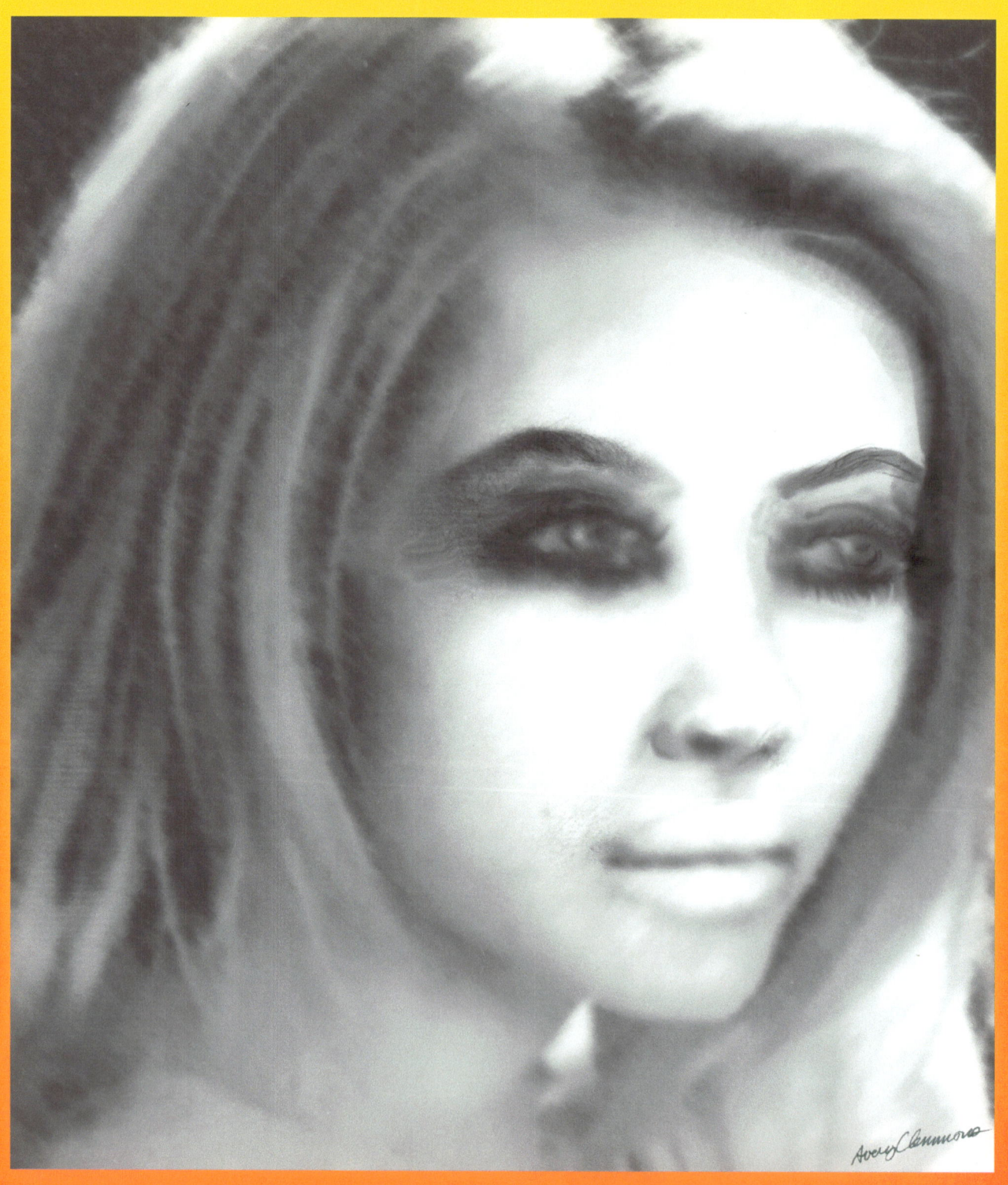

Angelina

This is an imagined portrait of a beautiful woman.

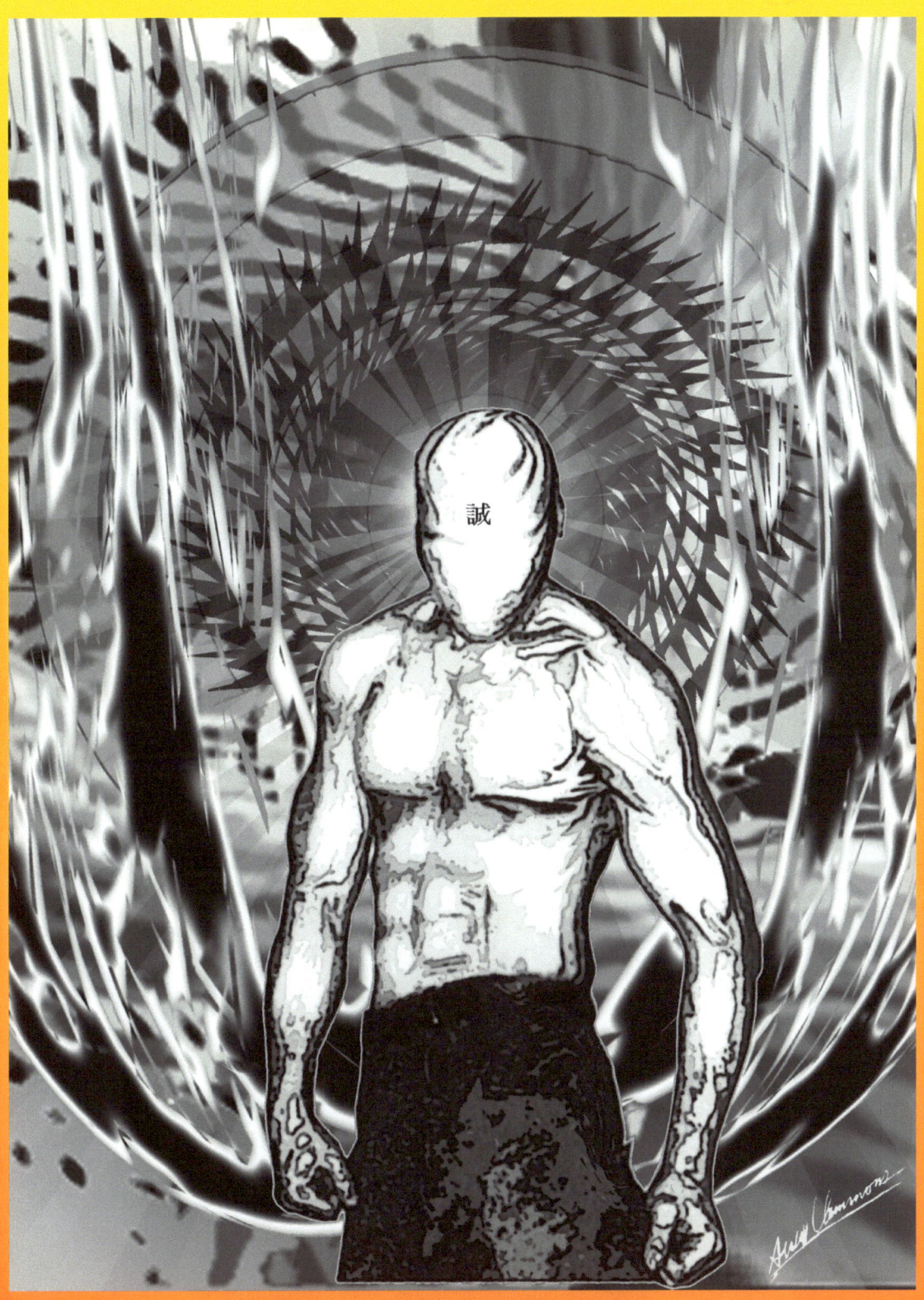

Black Hole Third Eye

A man stands in front of a black hole. In the black hole there is an Egyptian symbol that has a flaming appearance. This man uses the black hole to travel through time as a warrior, acquiring knowledge and strengths. He has a blank face, strong stance, and the symbol of integrity on the center of his forehead. The whole image signifies that any person can become wise and great using the wisdom of history and self discipline.

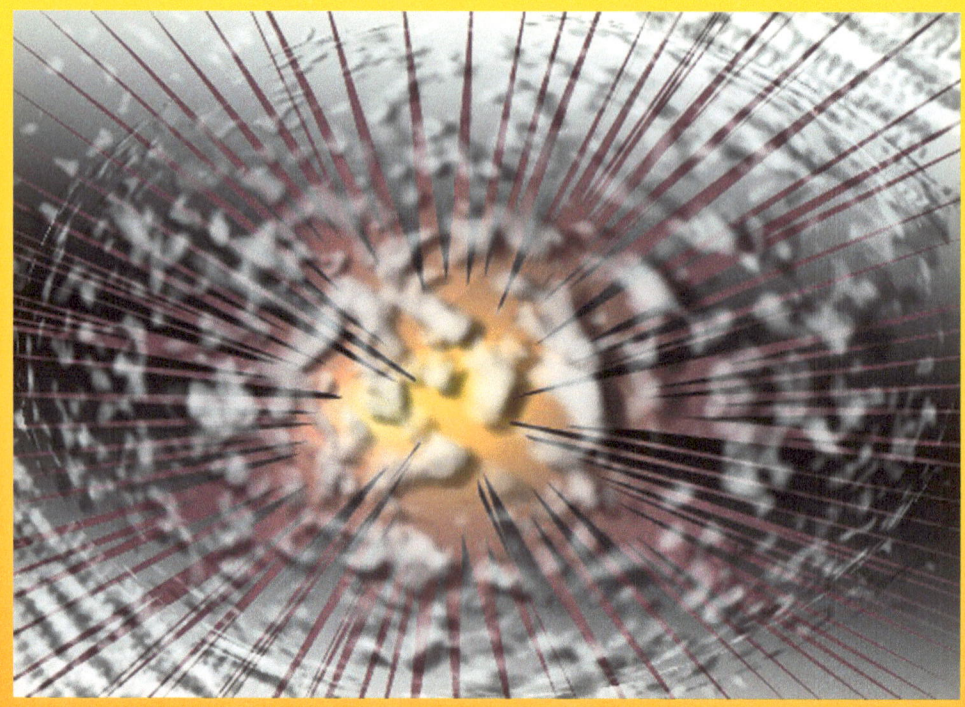

All un done

This explosion illuminated in the center with yellow and orange light is throwing gas, and splinters. It's such a powerful explosion that it ripples the atmosphere outwardly. This image makes a good background or wall hanging.

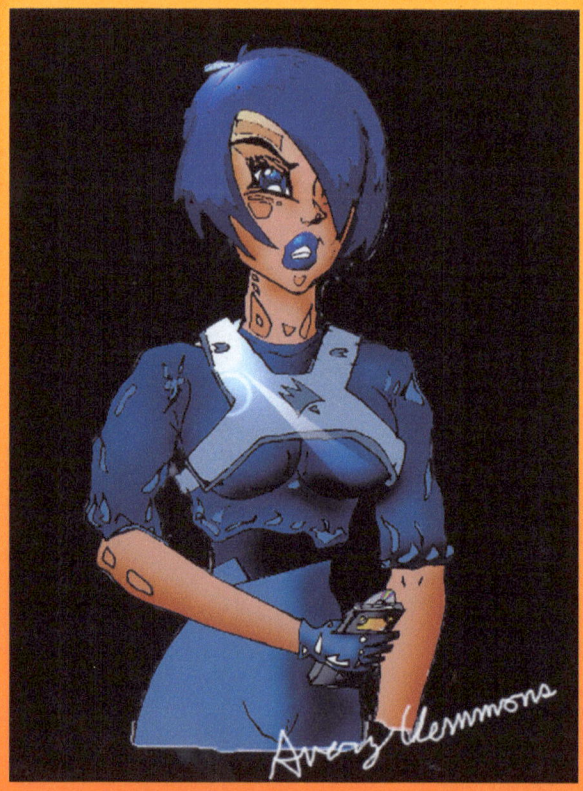

Warning in the Device

This is a woman that works as a special operative in law enforcement some time in the far future. The device she is holding warns her of any danger that might be in her area or approaching.

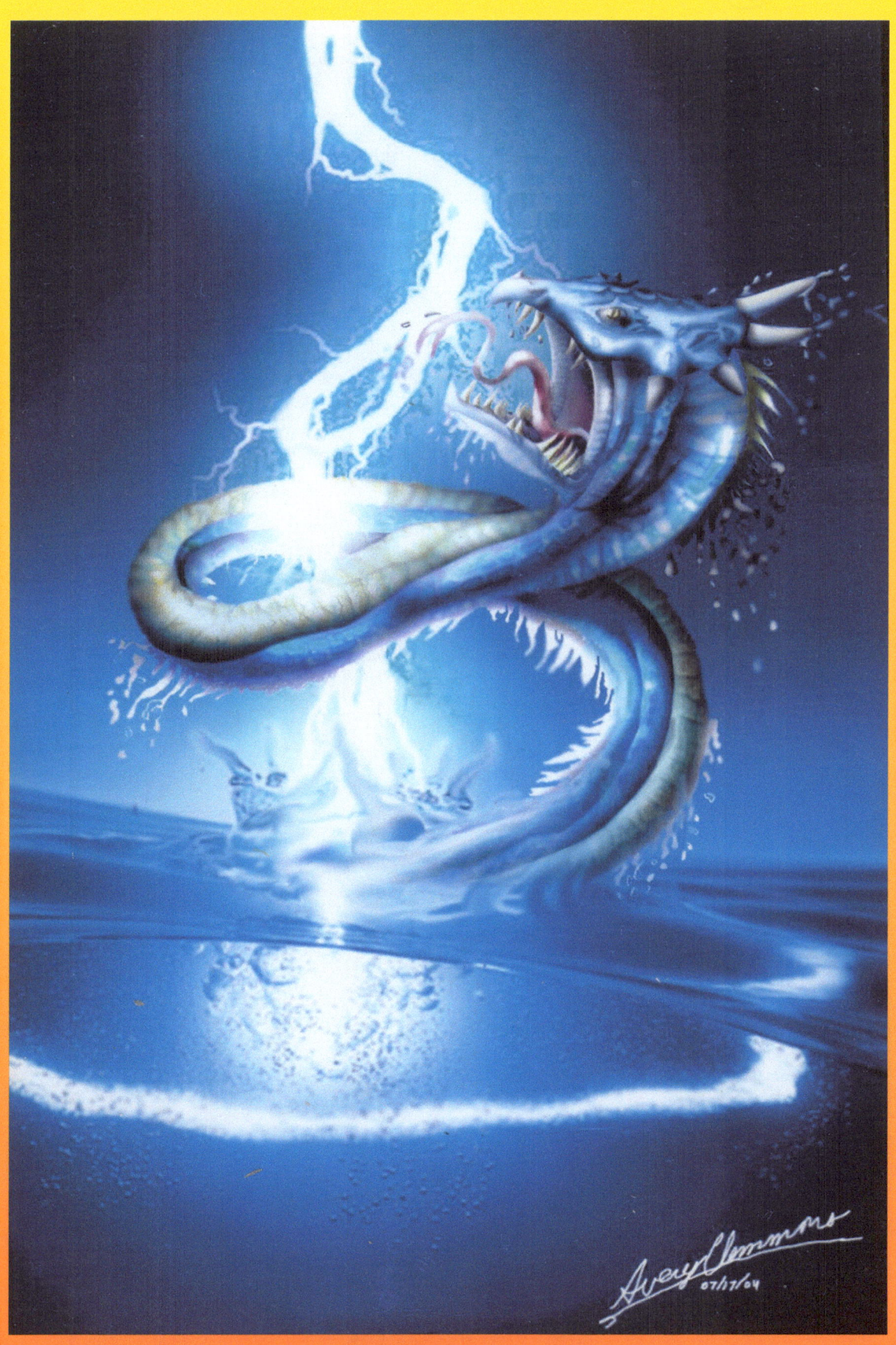

Blue Danger

Lightning, electricity, and the water elements give life to this serpent creature as it rises up and lashes its tongue at the lightning it has no fear of.

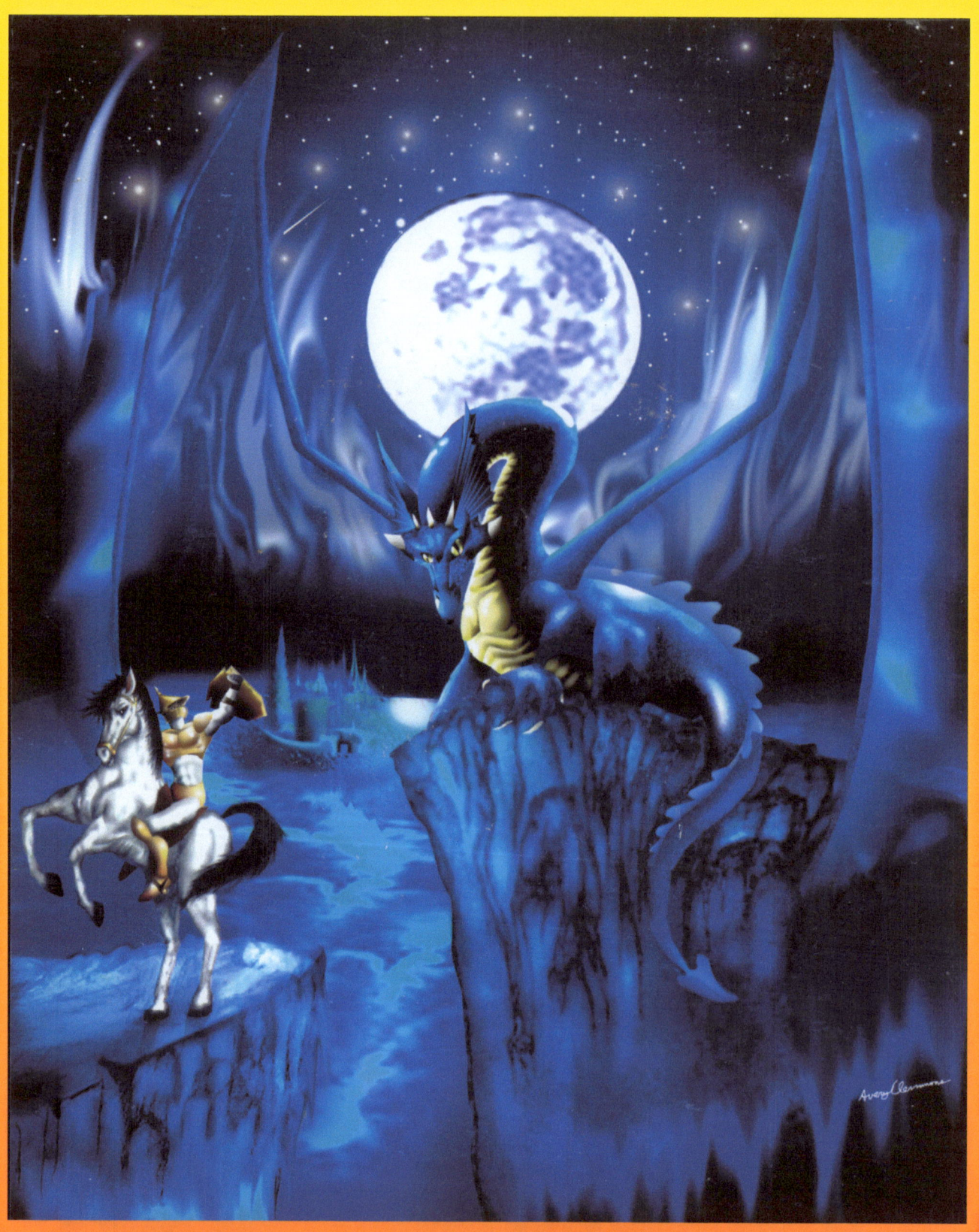

Knight

A picture of a hero clad in golden armor rides his loyal, white, stallion. He looks back into the moonlit night to see a ferocious dragon with massive wings waiting to attack. The hero knows that he can't defeat a dragon of this magnitude without help. He rears up on his horse raising his shield as he glances back in great fear. The theme of this painting is pick your battles wisely, and never face a dragon without a sword.

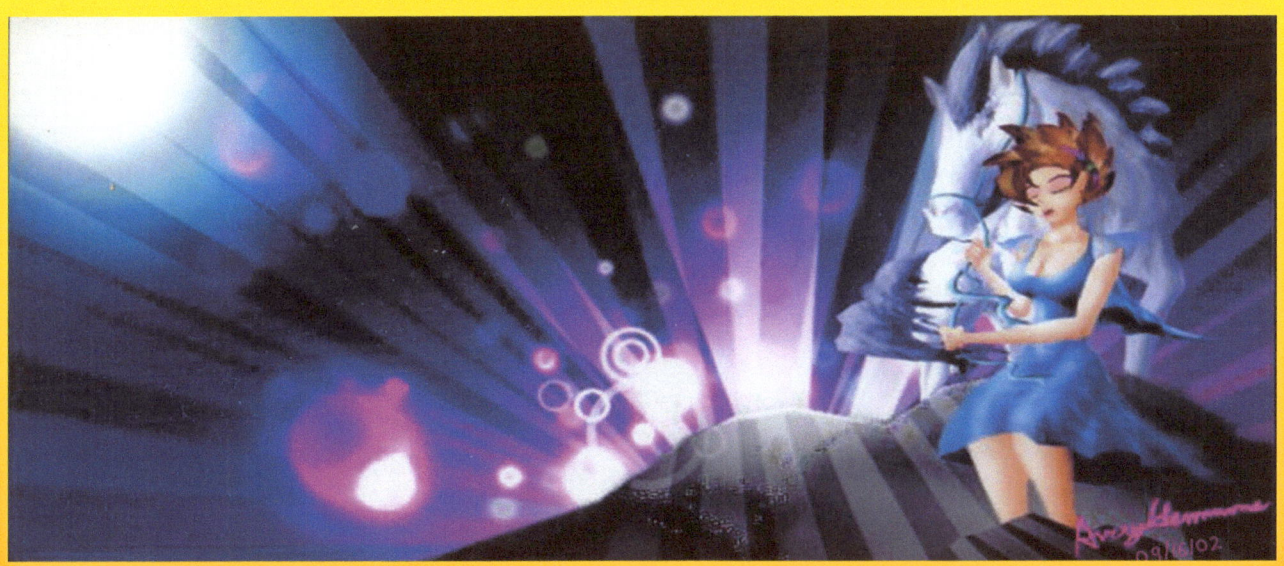

The Horses Glow

The Horse's Glow was created as a gift for a friend who loves horses and has a passion for riding.

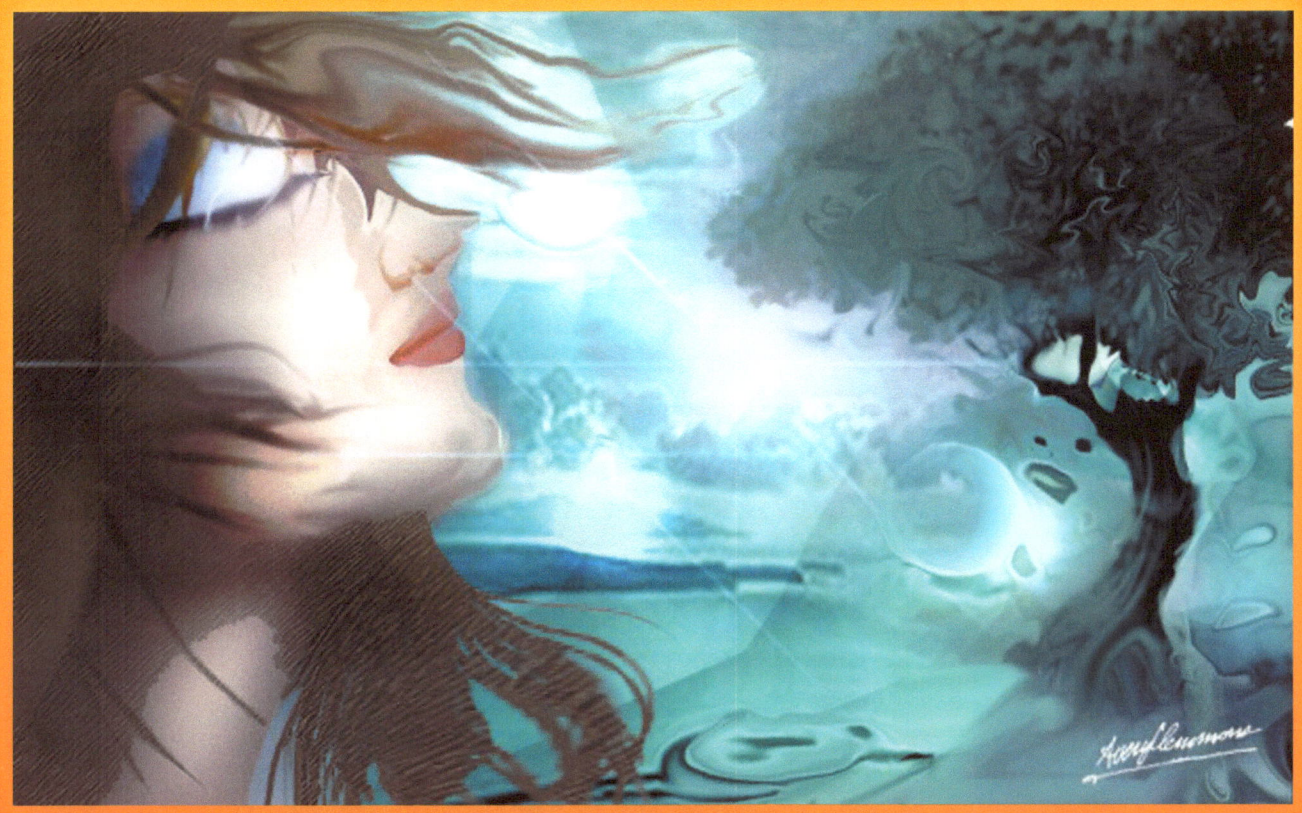

Dreaming

Wind blows through her hair reminding her of being on a beach. The woman closes her eyes and imagines. The scene seems real as rays of light flow from her day dream. In her mind she can see the ocean, a beautiful tree, and bright lights in the distance.

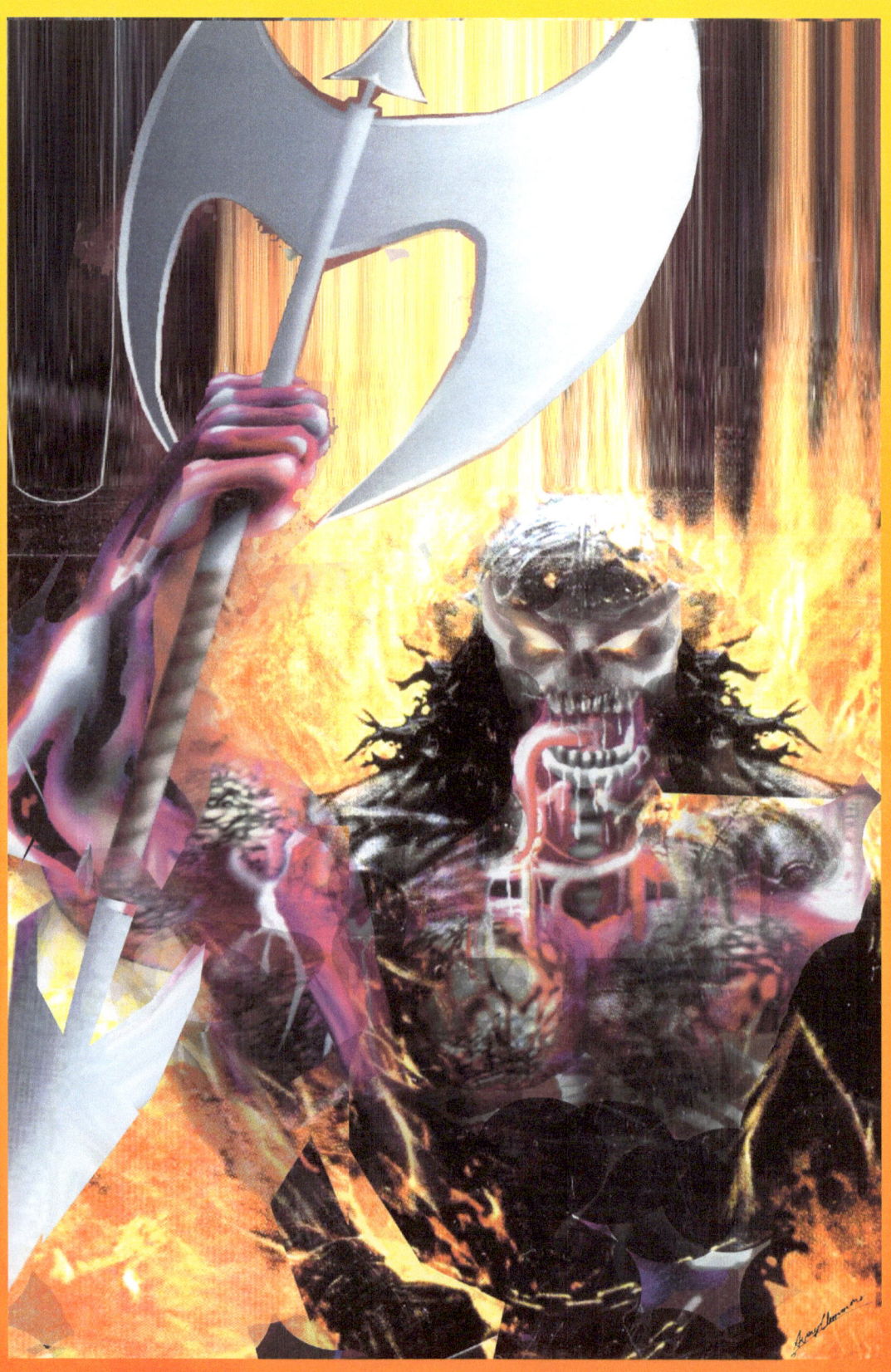

Him

Him is a demon creature that lives in Hell. He has no soul and a decayed heart full of hate. His tough body is covered with rottenness and exposed bones. With his lashing tongue he tells endless lies. His eyes are filled with flames. He is a member of the Dark Army, second in command, and has conquered many souls. His master is the Prince of Darkness himself. This monster wields a battle axe that can also be used as a spear.

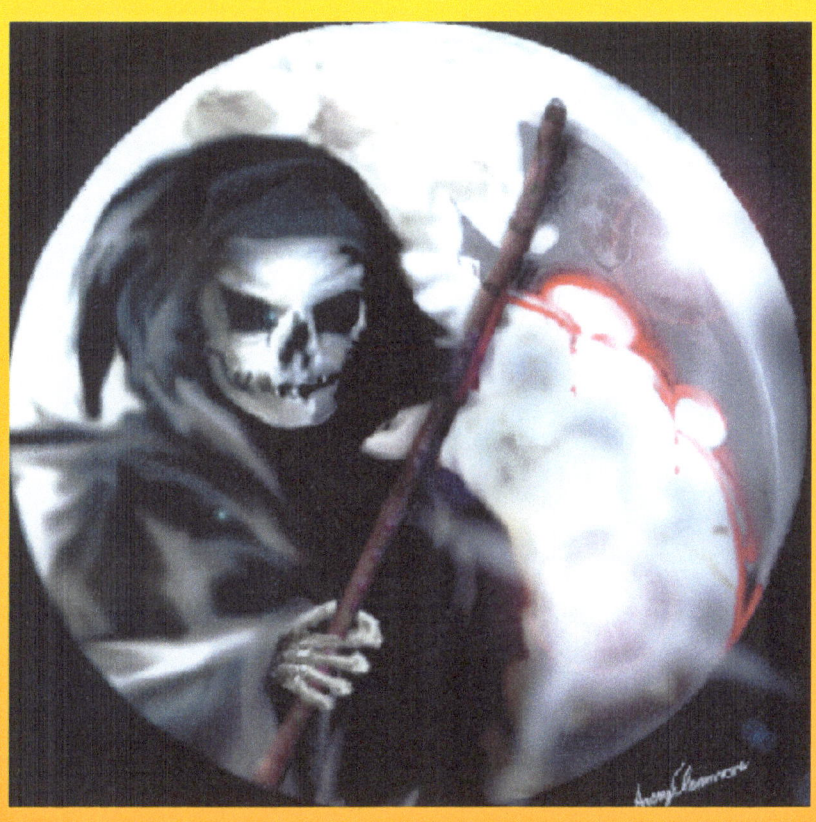

Moon Reaper

Moon Reaper is a drawing done for a friend that wanted it as a tattoo. The full moon is in the background and a reaper holds a jagged blood covered sickle that he uses to claim the dead souls.

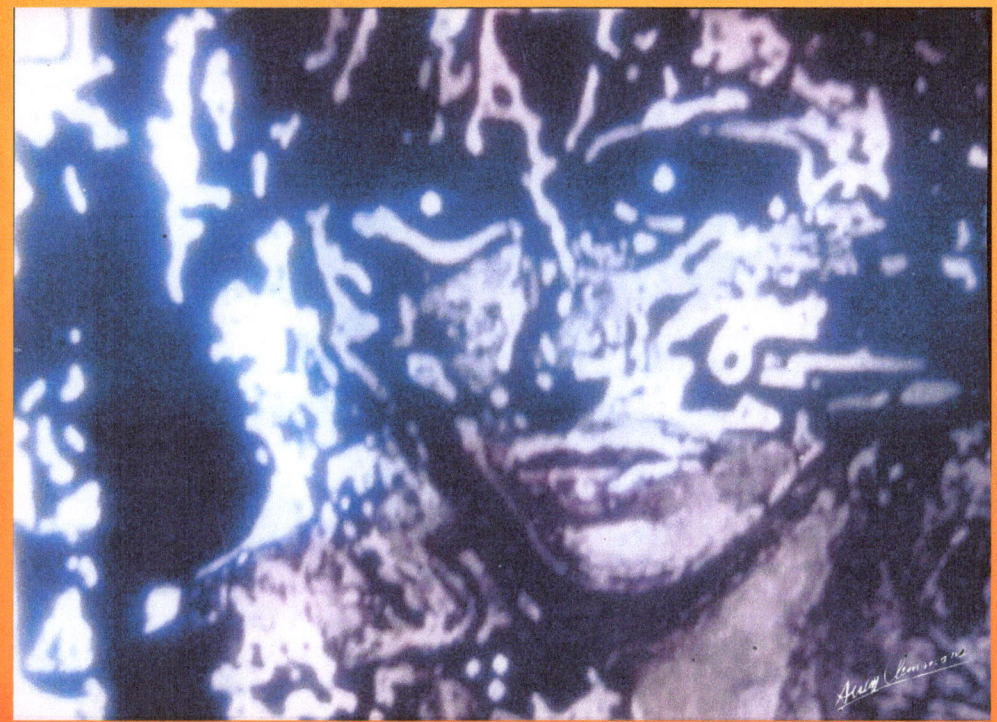

Melt and Condemn

Melt and Condemn is a judgmental and angry woman. She has a liquid look and few colors. There is a bright light that wont fill her dark, suffering eyes.

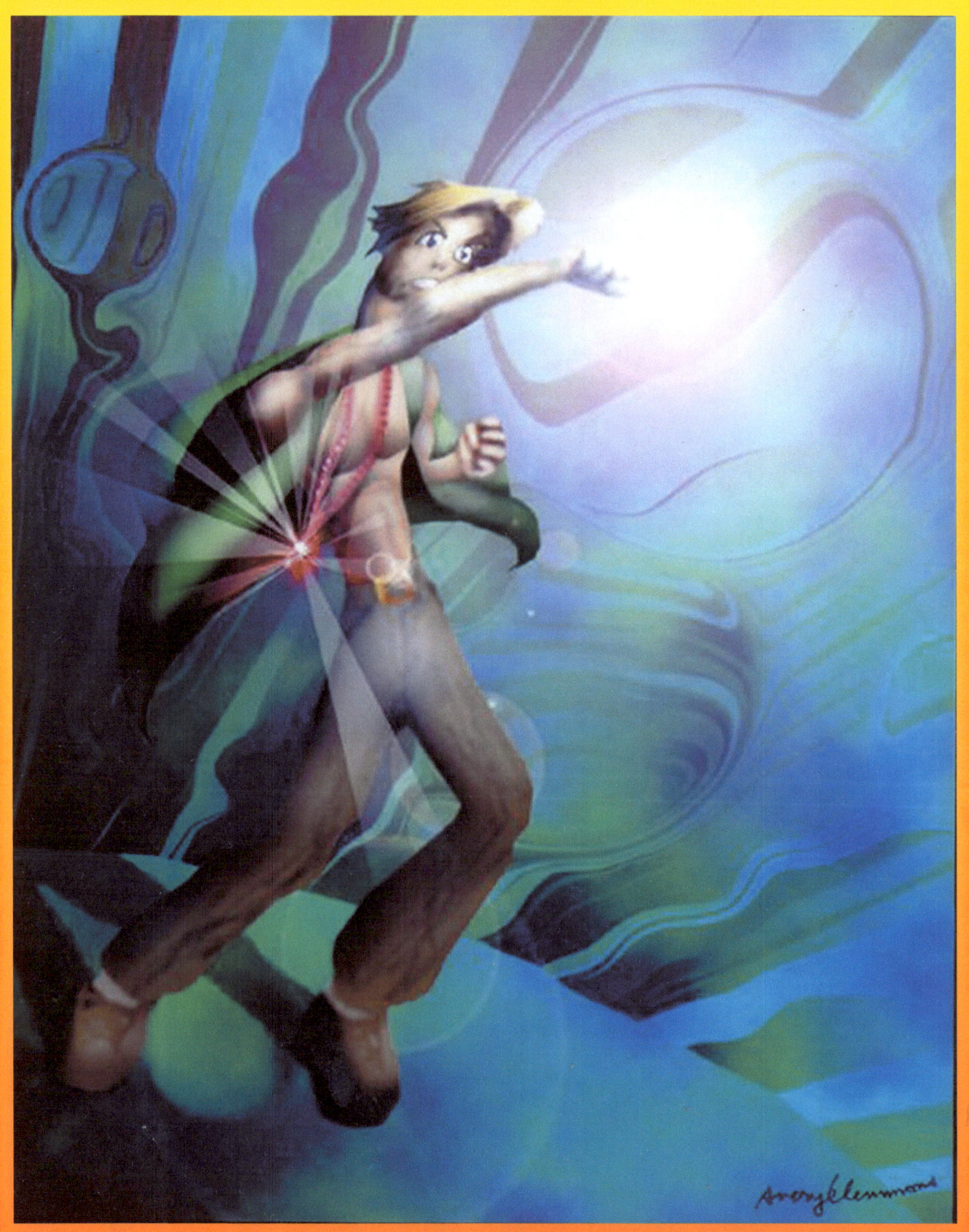

Rayhab

Rayhab is a young wizard in practice. Energy bursts from his right fist. He has a ruby jewel necklace that has magical power He needs this necklace to fulfill his destiny.

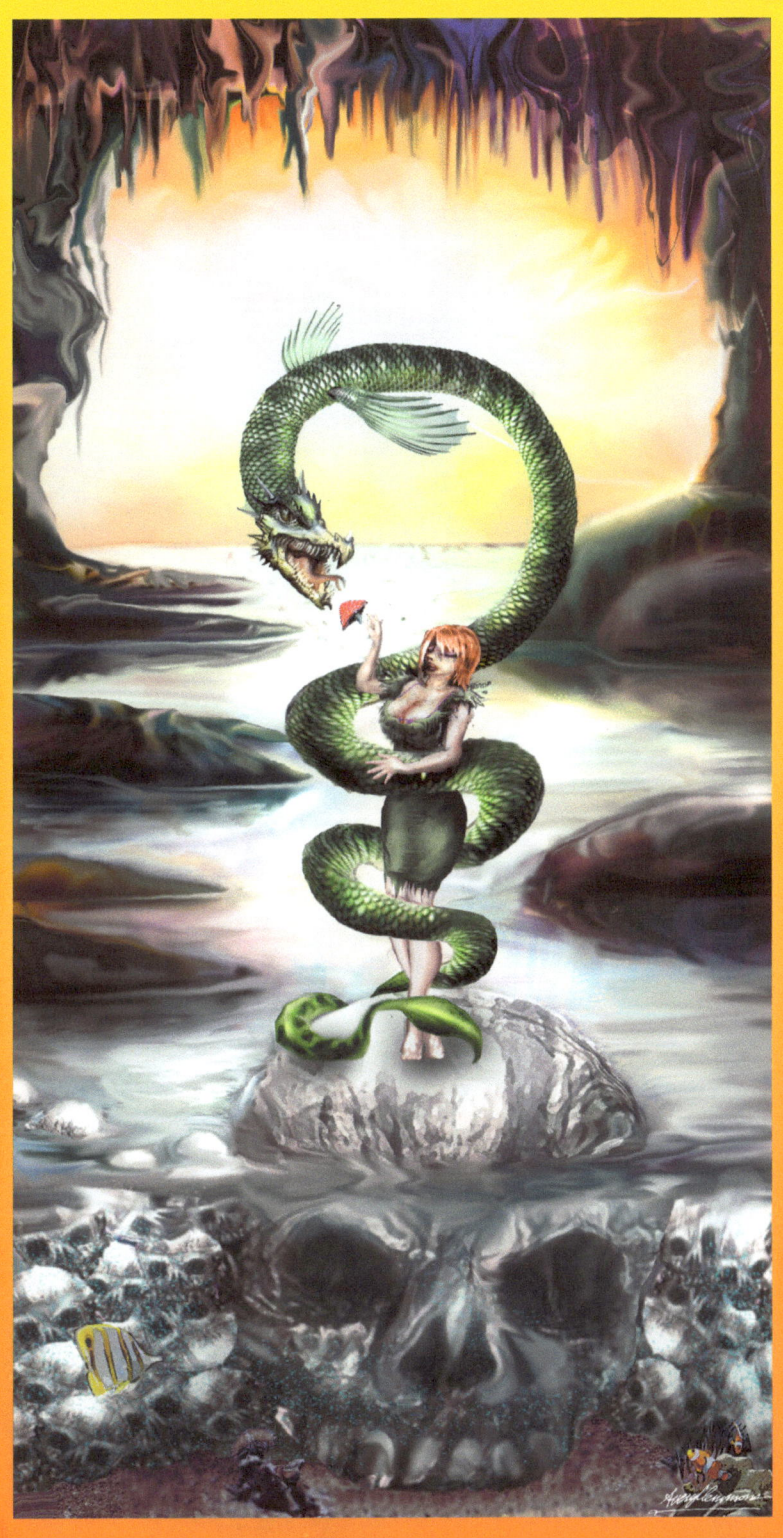

Taming

Taming is an imaginary place filled with stalactites. A river runs into an island cave from a nearby ocean in the distance, and winds down the center of the picture into a giant skull that is half buried and surrounded by many smaller skulls. On the top of the skulls stands a shipwrecked woman wearing a green, tattered, dress, entangled by a sea serpent ready to devour her. The woman enjoys the fact this serpent creature can't seem to resist the poisonous mushroom she holds in her right hand. With the mushroom she can conquer the serpent and live to survive on a very mysterious island.

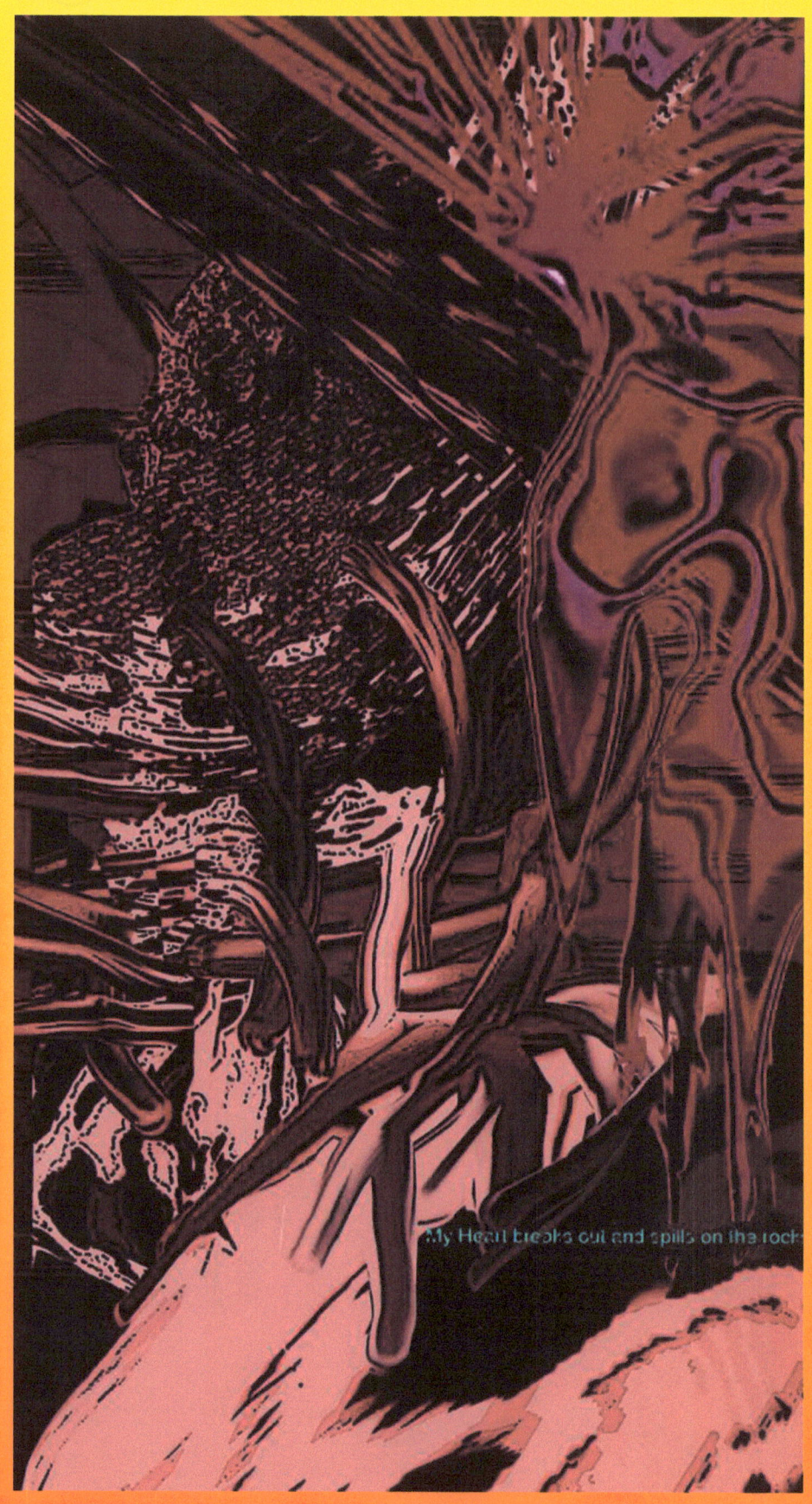

My Heart Breaks Out And Spills On The Rock

My Heart Breaks Out And Spills On The Rock is a painting that portrays the feelings of a broken heart.

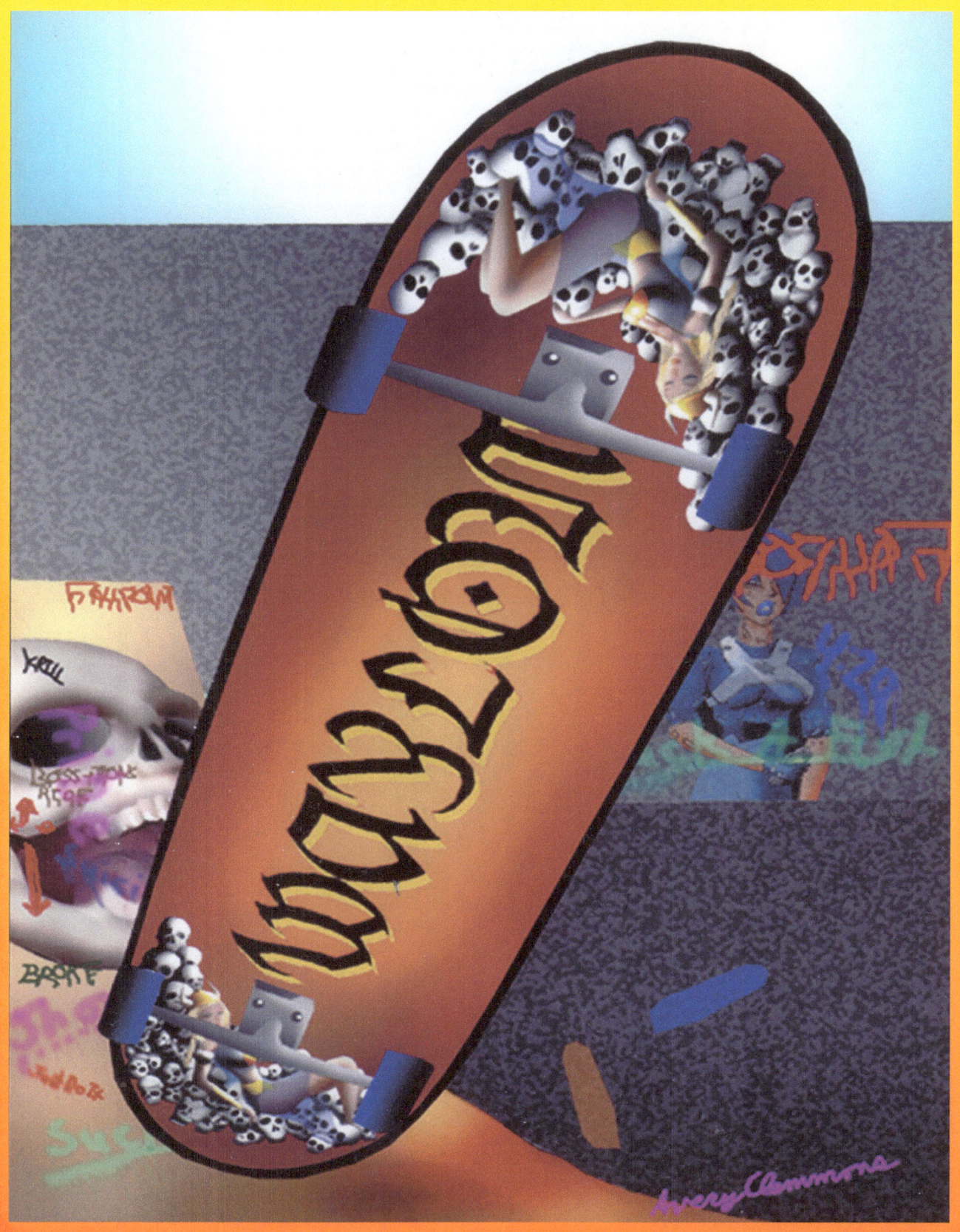

Waylon

Waylon was done for a friend who's son was killed in a terrible skateboarding accident. It is a memorial to her son. There is a skateboard with two identical images of a Viking woman lying on a pile off skulls.

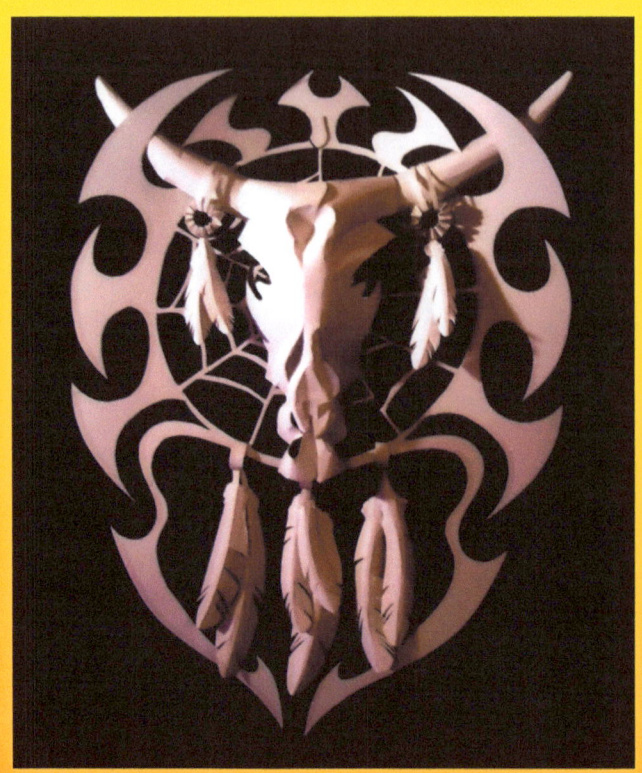

Bull Skull

Bull Skull one and two are very western in design. Sculpted out of heavy construction paper, and painted with water colors, is a bull's skull centered inside a sharp tribal design that circumferences the entire image. In the mid center is a circular spider's web that holds the skull in place. The bottom of the design has three sets of feathers attached hanging from their beaded quill tips.

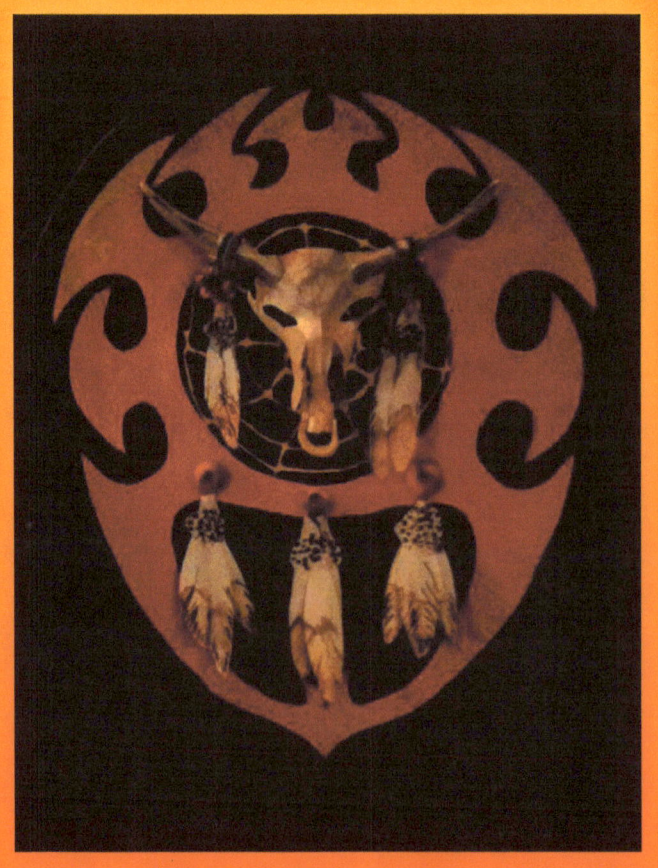

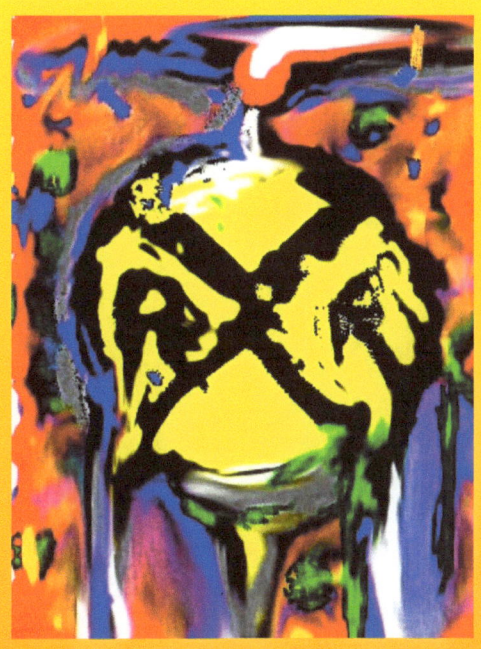

The Railroad crossing

The Railroad crossing is a finger-painting. This picture is a depiction of how I felt one day standing out in the rain waiting for the long train to pass. Cold and wet, I looked up at the sign. The red flashing light blares into my eyes as I sway to the left in anticipation of the passing train, keeping me from finding a more comfortable place. Emulating dreariness, the image is painted with a kind of melting, watery, and abstract affect.

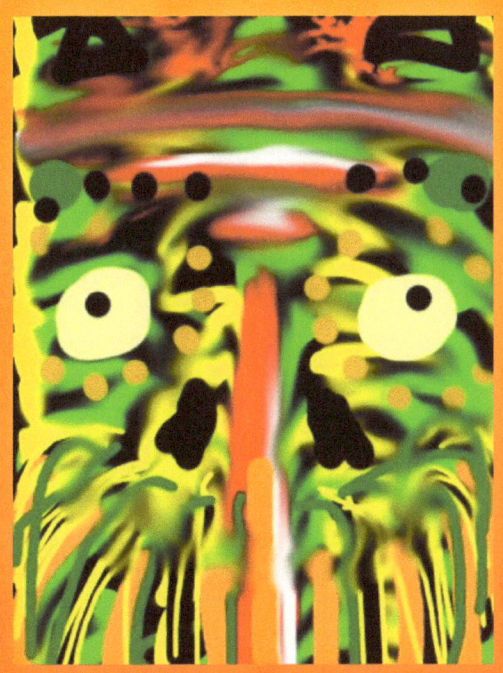

The O and B

The O and B is a finger-painting in abstract form. This image is simple and appears to have a set of eyes that look in different directions. There is a set of three red lines going across the top and dots of black and orange surrounding the eyes. Down the center of the image is another red line and on either side near the end are black smudges that end up at the bottom. Flowing streams of green, yellow, and orange make this painting look like it has a mouth or a mustache.

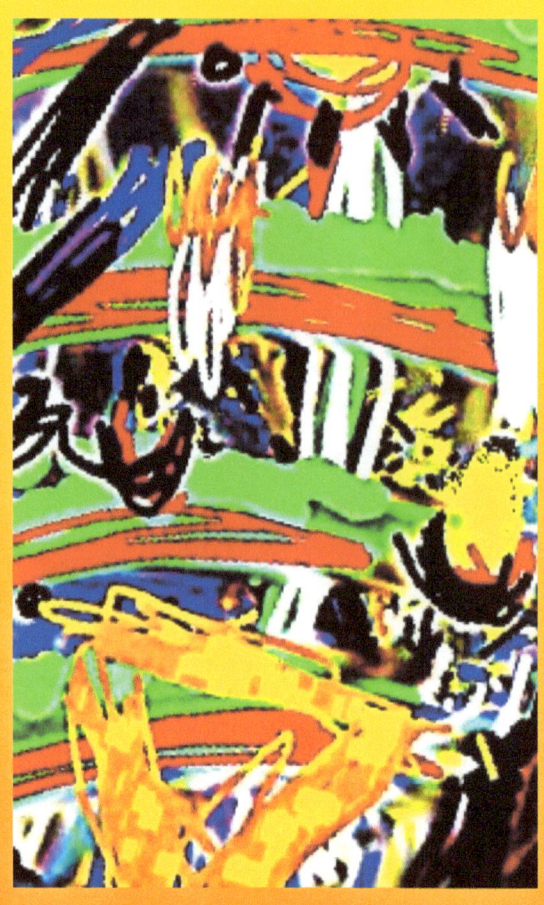

NACHOS

Nachos is a finger painting done in abstract form depicting the light, colors, movement, and feelings that you might find at a Mexican street party.

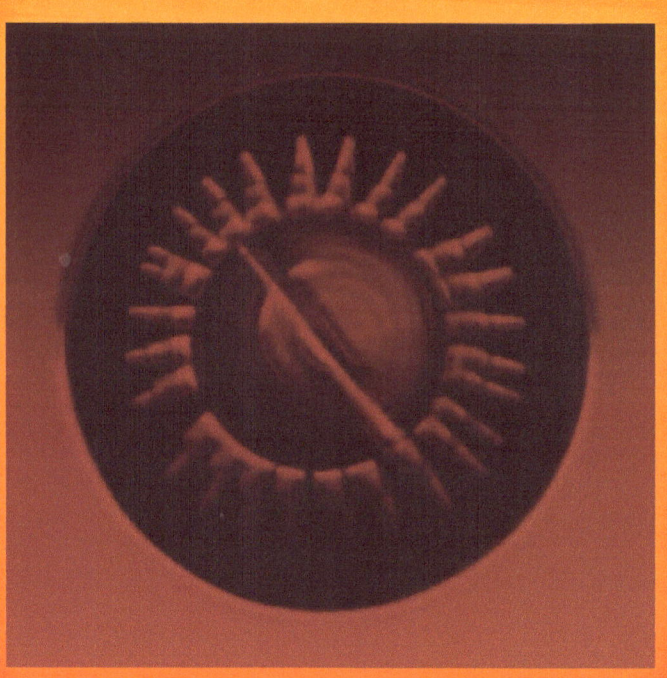

Screw top

Screw top is the most basic of mechanical design in abstract form.

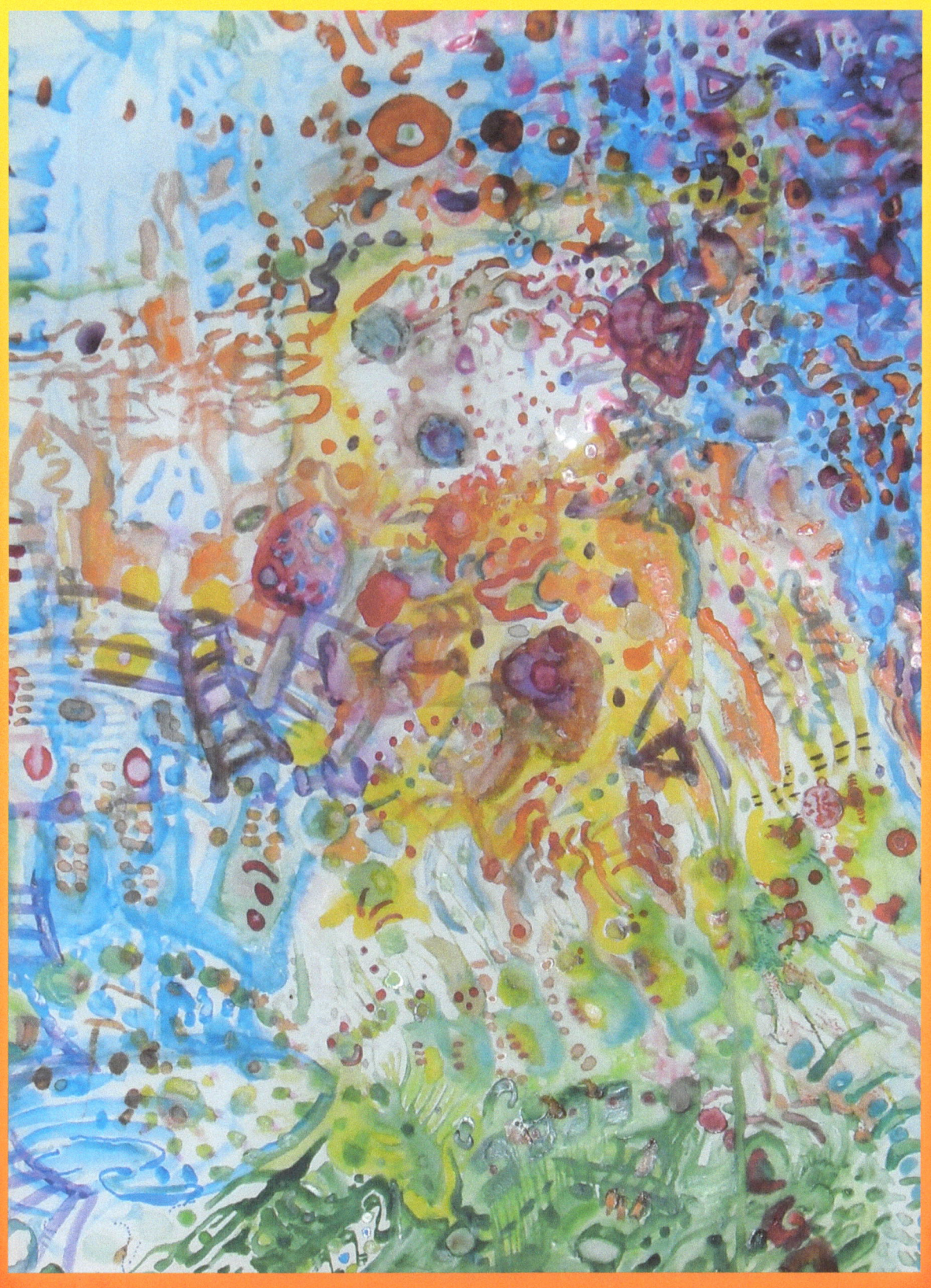

Mixer

This water color painting has many small symbols and characters floating around, portraying lots of meanings and expressions. Ladders, mushrooms and plants sort of wander everywhere. This mixed up image is painted in an Italian style of abstract.

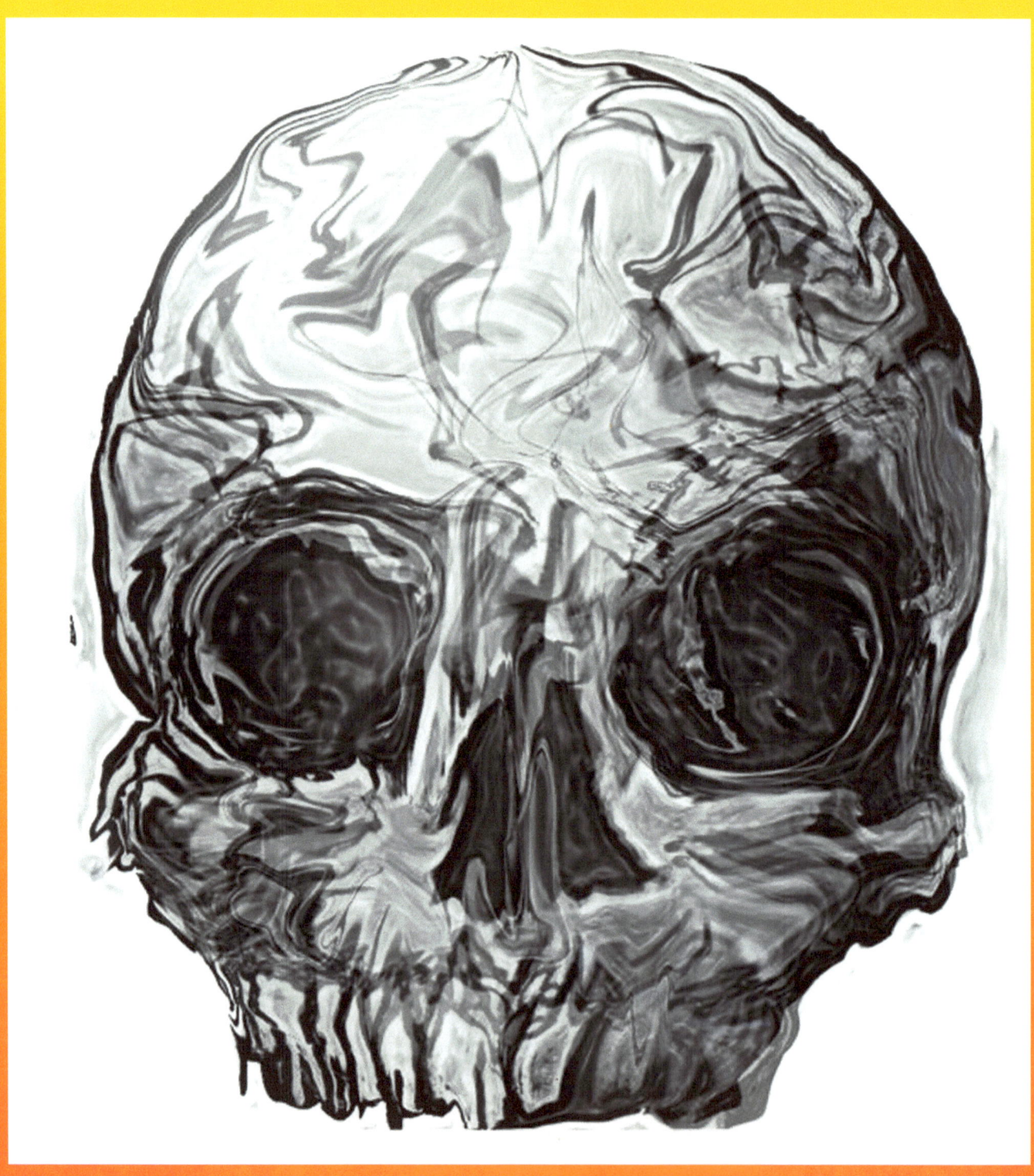

Smoke

Smoke is just a skull that I sketched and altered using computer generated filters to give it kind of a smoky look. After I altered this skull a few more times, I used it as the giant skull in the painting called Taming.